Minibeasts

Cheryl Palin

Contents

OXFORD
UNIVERSITY PRESS

OXFORD
UNIVERSITY PRESS

Great Clarendon Street, Oxford OX2 6DP

Oxford University Press is a department of the University of Oxford. It furthers the University's objective of excellence in research, scholarship, and education by publishing worldwide in

Oxford New York

Auckland Cape Town Dar es Salaam Hong Kong Karachi Kuala Lumpur Madrid Melbourne Mexico City Nairobi New Delhi Shanghai Taipei Toronto

With offices in

Argentina Austria Brazil Chile Czech Republic France Greece Guatemala Hungary Italy Japan Poland Portugal Singapore South Korea Switzerland Thailand Turkey Ukraine Vietnam

OXFORD and OXFORD ENGLISH are registered trade marks of Oxford University Press in the UK and in certain other countries

ISBN: 978 0 19 464379 5

An Audio CD Pack containing this book and a CD is also available
ISBN: 978 019 464419 8

The CD has a choice of American and British English recordings of the complete text.

An accompanying Activity Book is also available
ISBN: 978 0 19 464389 4

Printed in China

ACKNOWLEDGEMENTS

Illustrations by: Fiammetta Dogi/The Art Agency pp4, 5, 6, 9, 22, 25, 32 (worm, scorpion, fly, slug, beetle), 36, 39; Alan Rowe pp32 (leaves, soil, butterfly, egg), 34, 38, 40, 46, 47; Gary Swift pp7, 19.

The Publishers would also like to thank the following for their kind permission to reproduce photographs and other copyright material: Alamy pp6 (Juniors Bildarchiv), 8 (Andrew Darrington), 9 (Robert Pickett/Papilio), 10 (Graphic Science), 12 (Matt Meadows/Peter Arnold, Inc), 13 (Custom Life Science Images/caterpillar, egg, pupa, butterfly on flower), 15 (Blickwinkel/Wothe), 16 (Derek Croucher), 17 (Fritz Poelking/Elvele Images Ltd), 22 (Phil Degginger), 23 (Fritz Poelking/Evele Images Ltd), 28 (Andrew Darrington), 33 (Custon Life Science Images); Corbis pp11 (ants/Klaus Honel/Naturfoto Honel), 18 (Joe MacDonald), 21 (© CDC/PHIL); Getty Images pp14 (Hashim/Gulf Images/date), 20 (Vincenzo Lombardo/Taxi/fig), 24 (Andy Crawford/Dorling Kindersley/give), 30 (Mark Moffett/Minden Pictures/insect), 32 (Philip J Brittan/Photonica/kick), 64 (Andy Crawford/Dorling Kindersley/zero); Oxford University Press pp3, 7, 13 (butterfly), 14, 19, 26; Photolibrary pp11 (fireflies), 16 (snail); Barbara Strnadova/www.godofinsects.com pp20.

Introduction

spider

There are millions of different types of minibeast. They can be many different shapes and sizes. Some are very small, some are colorful, and some have lots of legs. They live in different places all over the world!

scorpion

bee

butterfly

What minibeasts do you know?
How many legs does a butterfly have?
How many eyes does a spider have?
Which minibeast has a home on its back?

snail

Discover!
Now read and discover more about amazing minibeasts!

Minibeasts

A minibeast is a small animal with no backbone. It's an invertebrate. There are many different types of minibeast. Scientists put them into different groups.

The biggest group is the arthropods. Arthropods have six or more legs. Some arthropods are insects. Insects have six legs. There are more than one million types of insect. Some examples are bees, beetles, ants, flies, and grasshoppers.

Types of Minibeast

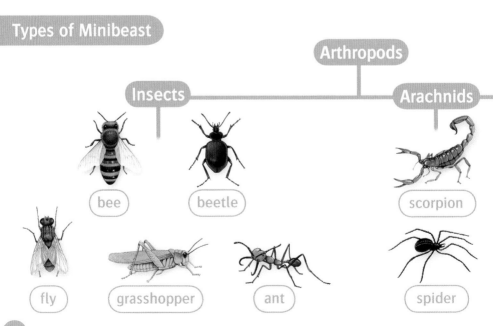

Arthropods

Insects

Arachnids

bee

beetle

scorpion

fly

grasshopper

ant

spider

Some arthropods are arachnids. Arachnids have eight legs. Scorpions and spiders are arachnids.

Some arthropods are myriapods. They have lots of legs. Centipedes and millipedes are myriapods. Centipedes have two legs on each body section. Millipedes have four legs on each body section.

Some minibeasts don't have legs. Snails and slugs don't have legs. They are molluscs. Earthworms and leeches don't have legs. Their bodies have lots of sections. They are annelids. Which minibeasts do you know?

Myriapods

centipede

millipede

Molluscs

snail

slug

Annelids

earthworm

leech

➡ Go to pages 24–25 for activities.

Insect Bodies

Most insect bodies have three parts: a head, a thorax, and an abdomen. The head has eyes and a mouth. The thorax has legs and wings.

A Wasp

wings

thorax

head

abdomen

eyes

legs

mouth

Insects don't have any bones, but they have a hard cover. This hard cover is called an exoskeleton. Insects grow, but their exoskeleton can't grow. When an exoskeleton is too small, it comes off. Then the insect grows a new, bigger exoskeleton.

small cicada

exoskeleton

bigger cicada

Insects can use their bodies to hide from birds and other animals. They don't want the other animals to eat them. This is called camouflage.

A Camouflaged Leaf Insect

Discover!

Some insects have bright colors. Animals don't eat any insect that is black, white, and red. It isn't usually good to eat. Sometimes it's poisonous.

Go to pages 26–27 for activities.

Insect Senses

Most insects have two very big eyes. They can't see clearly, but they can see things move very well. Some insects have extra eyes that can only see light and dark.

A Hornet

extra eyes

antennae

big eyes

Some minibeasts have antennae on their head. They use their antennae to feel and touch things. They can also smell food and other minibeasts with their antennae.

Butterflies have a very long tongue called a proboscis. They use their tongue to taste and drink nectar in flowers. Butterflies can also taste with their feet!

A Butterfly

proboscis

Most insects don't have ears on their head. Do you know where they are? They have ears on their body or their legs!

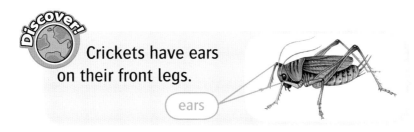

Discover!

Crickets have ears on their front legs.

ears

Go to pages 28–29 for activities.

4 Communication

Most male and female minibeasts communicate with each other because they need to make new, baby minibeasts!

Some minibeasts communicate with sound. Grasshoppers can sing. They move their legs up and down to make a singing sound.

Some minibeasts communicate with smell. The female moth makes strong smells called pheromones. The male moth can smell the female with its antennae.

A Male Emperor Moth

antennae

Discover!

The male emperor moth can smell a female 10 kilometers away!

Some minibeasts communicate with light. Fireflies can make light with their abdomen. Male and female fireflies flash their lights to each other.

Some minibeasts communicate to give each other information. Bees dance to tell other bees where there is food. Ants touch each other's antennae or head to give information about food or danger.

Ants

Go to pages 30–31 for activities.

Baby Minibeasts

Most baby minibeasts come from eggs. Some minibeasts, like slugs and earthworms, lay their eggs in soil. Other minibeasts, like butterflies and beetles, lay their eggs on plants.

Scorpions don't lay eggs. They have live babies. The baby scorpions travel on their mother's back.

A Female Scorpion and Babies

The babies of some flying insects look like their parents, but they don't have any wings. Baby grasshoppers don't have any wings. They grow wings when they get bigger.

Some babies are larvae. Beetle, butterfly, and bee babies are larvae. After a few weeks, they become pupae. Then they become insects with wings, like their parents.

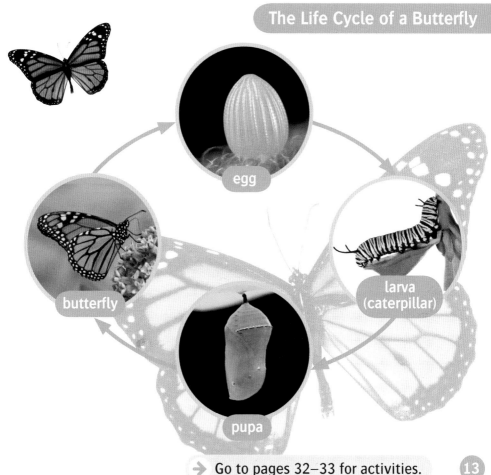

The Life Cycle of a Butterfly

egg

larva (caterpillar)

pupa

butterfly

→ Go to pages 32–33 for activities.

Working Insects

Some insects work together in groups. Leafcutter ants work together. First they find leaves. They carry the leaves to their nest. Fungus grows from the leaves, and then the ants eat the fungus.

Leafcutter Ants

Discover!

Leafcutter ants are very strong. They can carry leaves that are about 50 times heavier than their bodies!

queen bee

female worker bees

honeycomb

Honeybees work together, too. One queen bee lays all the eggs. Then the female worker bees care for the bee larvae. They look for food, they make honey from nectar, and they give honey to the bee larvae. They keep the honey in honeycombs inside the hive. The worker bees also clean the hive.

→ Go to pages 34–35 for activities.

15

A Dragonfly

A Snail

Some minibeasts, like earthworms and ants, live underground, and others live in water. Dragonflies lay their eggs on leaves in the water. Their larvae live underwater.

Snails carry their home on their back. They live in many different places. Land snails live in deserts, mountains, forests, and gardens. Marine snails live in the ocean.

Lots of minibeasts make nests. Some wasps make nests from wasp paper. They make the paper from wood and saliva. The queen wasp lays eggs in the nest. The nest has lots of small rooms for the wasp larvae. Wasps attack other animals to protect their nest.

A Wasp Nest

Discover!

A wasp nest can have about 10,000 wasps inside!

Go to pages 36–37 for activities.

Spiders

Spiders have two body parts and eight legs. They have six or eight eyes.

All spiders can make silk. Some spiders use the silk to make webs. Insects fly into the web. Then the spider eats the insects.

Some spiders hunt. The wolf spider hides in leaves. Then it jumps out and catches insects, mice, and frogs.

A Wolf Spider

A spider can only eat liquid food. It bites an animal with a poison that makes the animal liquid inside. Then the spider drinks the liquid.

Female spiders are often much bigger than male spiders.

A Spider Eating an Insect in a Web

Discover!

The Golden Orb female spider can have a body up to ten times bigger than the male!

Go to pages 38–39 for activities.

Problems with Minibeasts

Some minibeasts can sting. The part that can sting is called a stinger. A wasp and an ant can sting again and again. A bee can only sting once. Then it dies.

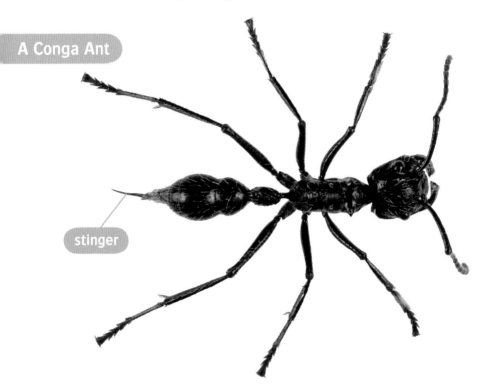

A Conga Ant

stinger

Other minibeasts can bite. Some spiders have a poisonous bite, and other animals can die from this poison. A person can die from the bite of a black widow spider.

Discover!

Only female mosquitoes bite.

Minibeasts can also make people sick. They can bite people and give them diseases. Mosquitoes can give people a very bad disease called malaria.

Some minibeasts make problems for farmers. Locusts are a type of grasshopper. They eat a lot of food crops. Other minibeasts make problems in our homes. Some moths eat clothes, and some beetles eat wood.

➜ Go to pages 40–41 for activities.

Useful Minibeasts

Minibeasts are important food for many other animals. Fish, frogs, bats, and birds eat minibeasts.

Insects help plants grow. Insects visit different flowers to collect food. The pollen from one flower sticks to the body of the insect. When the insect goes to another flower, the pollen falls onto this flower. The flower uses this pollen to make seeds. Then a new plant grows. This is called pollination.

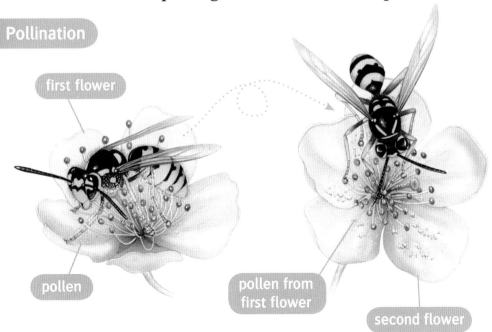

Pollination

first flower

pollen

pollen from first flower

second flower

Earthworms help soil and plants. When they move through the soil, they let air and water in. Plant roots need the air and water.

An Earthworm

Bees give us honey and silkworms give us silk. Silkworms make silk cocoons when they become pupae. People use silkworm cocoons to make silk fabric.

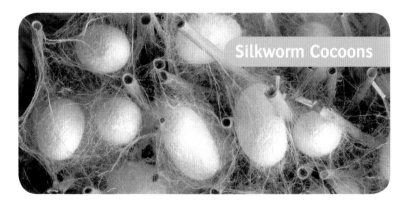

Silkworm Cocoons

Minibeasts are amazing. They are also very useful! People, animals, and plants all need minibeasts to live.

➔ Go to activities on pages 42–43.

1 Minibeasts

← Read pages 4–5.

1 **Complete the chart.**

leech ~~grasshopper~~ millipede fly centipede snail
bee ant spider slug earthworm beetle scorpion

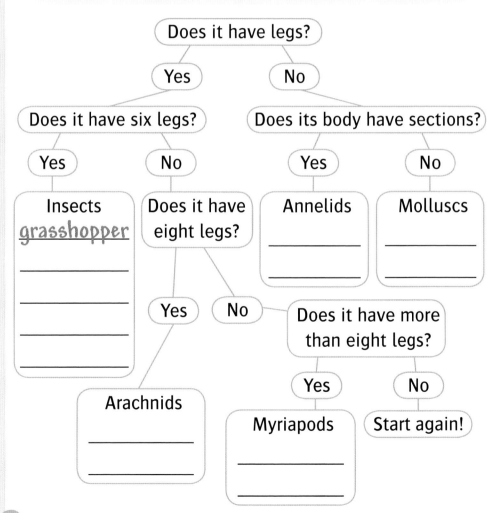

2 Match. Then write the words.

1 It has six legs. It has wings.
It's black and yellow.
It's an insect.

_____

2 It has eight legs. It has a tail.
It's an arachnid.

_____

3 It doesn't have legs.
It has a shell. It's a mollusc.

_bee_____

4 It doesn't have legs.
It doesn't have a shell.
It's an annelid.

_____

3 Draw and write about two minibeasts.

This is a _____

It has_____

It has_____

It's _____

It's _____

_____

_____

_____

_____

_____

25

2 Insect Bodies

← Read pages 6–7.

1 Write the words.

head
thorax
abdomen
leg
wing

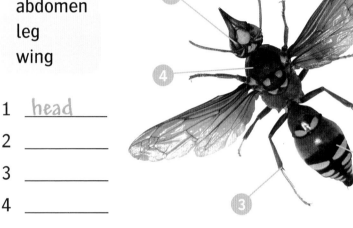

1 head
2 _____
3 _____
4 _____
5 _____

2 Complete the sentences.

cover   small   new   ~~bones~~   grow

Insects don't have any _bones_ . They have a hard

_____ called an exoskeleton. Insects _____,

but their exoskeletons can't grow. When an

exoskeleton is too _____ , it comes off. Then

the insect grows a _____ , bigger exoskeleton.

3 Circle the correct words.

1 Insects (can) / can't use their body to hide.

2 Insects **want** / **don't want** other animals to eat them.

3 **Some** / **All** insect bodies are camouflaged.

4 An insect that is black, white, and red **is** / **isn't** good to eat.

5 Insects are **sometimes** / **never** poisonous.

6 An exoskeleton **can** / **can't** grow.

4 Answer the questions.

1 What color are insects that are not good to eat?

_____

2 How many parts do most insects have?

_____

3 What are the names of the insect parts?

_____

4 What happens when an exoskeleton is too small?

_____

5 How do insects hide from other animals?

_____

3 Insect Senses

← Read pages 8–9.

1 Write *true* or *false*.

1 All insects have only two eyes. _false_

2 Some insects have more than two eyes. _____

3 Insects can see very clearly. _____

4 Insects can see things move. _____

5 All insects see light and dark. _____

6 Most insects have ears on their head. _____

2 Write the sentences.

These are antennae.
These eyes can see things move.
These eyes can see light and dark.

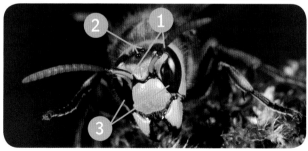

1 _____

2 _____

3 _____

3 **Write *People, Insects,* or *People and insects*.**

1 _____Insects_____ smell with their antennae.

2 _____ touch with their antennae.

3 _____ touch with their hands.

4 _____ taste with their feet.

5 _____ hear with their legs.

6 _____ see with their eyes.

4 **Draw and write about two insects.**

This is a _____

It has _____

It can _____

_____

It can _____

_____

_____

_____

_____

_____

_____

_____

4 Communication

← Read pages 10–11.

1 Find and write the minibeasts. Then draw them.

s	o	s	t	m	o	t	h	s	a	n	f
i	r	e	i	o	s	h	b	a	r	i	i
t	i	a	n	t	s	n	e	g	e	b	r
e	f	d	s	j	e	e	e	u	m	e	e
n	r	a	p	p	l	s	s	r	a	g	f
t	o	d	a	s	h	i	p	e	r	b	l
i	h	e	s	b	v	o	i	r	u	l	i
r	i	m	m	l	o	r	z	a	z	o	e
g	r	a	s	s	h	o	p	p	e	r	s

1 ___moths___

2 _____

3 _____   4 _____   5 _____

2 Write *male* or *female*.

The _____ moth makes strong smells called
pheromones. The _____ moth can smell the
_____ moth with its antennae. The _____
emperor moth can smell a _____ moth
10 kilometers away!

3 Find and write the words.

ontouchchdancetsmelllchsoundanlightononsing

1 _____ 2 _____ 3 _____

4 _____ 5 _____ 6 _____

4 Complete the sentences.

Bees Ants Grasshoppers Moths Fireflies

1 _____ communicate with smell.

2 _____ communicate with light.

3 _____ communicate with dance.

4 _____ communicate with sound.

5 _____ communicate with touch.

5 Answer the questions.

1 How do grasshoppers communicate?

_____

2 How do fireflies communicate?

_____

3 How do bees communicate?

_____

5 Baby Minibeasts

← Read pages 12–13.

1 Complete the puzzle. Write the secret word.

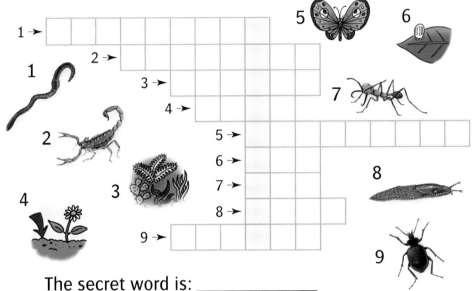

The secret word is: _____

2 Write ✔ or ✗

1 Most minibeasts
   lay eggs. ☐
   have live babies. ☐

2 Slugs and earthworms
   lay eggs
   in soil. ☐
   on plants. ☐

3 Butterflies and
   beetles lay eggs
   in soil. ☐
   on plants. ☐

4 Scorpions
   lay eggs. ☐
   have live babies. ☐

3 **Complete the diagram. Then write about the life cycle of a butterfly.**

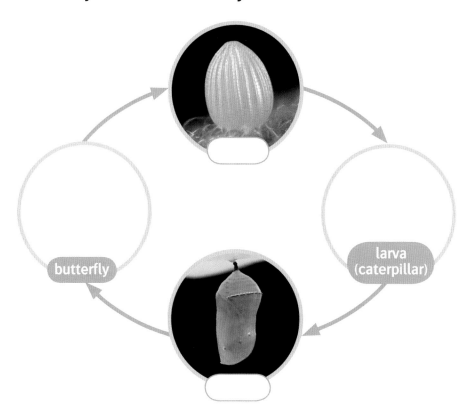

caterpillar   pupa   butterfly   wings   eggs
pupa   butterfly   caterpillar   insect

A _____ lays _____ . A _____
comes out of an egg. The _____ grows and it
becomes a _____ . Then a _____
comes out of the _____ . Now it's an
_____ with _____ .

6 Working Insects

← Read pages 14–15.

1 Number the sentences in order. Then write.

- ☐ Fungus grows.
- ☐ They carry the leaves to their nest.
- ☐ The leafcutter ants find leaves.
- ☐ They eat the fungus.

_____

_____

_____

_____

_____

_____

_____

_____

2 Write *true* or *false*.

1 Two queen bees lay the eggs.   _____

2 The workers are male.   _____

3 The workers care for the bee larvae.   _____

4 Bees make honey from nectar.   _____

5 Bees keep the honey in honeycombs.   _____

3 Complete the chart.

They live in a hive.   They are insects.
They carry leaves.   They keep honey in honeycombs.
They make honey.   They eat fungus.
They find leaves.   They work together in groups.

Leafcutter ants	_____ _____ _____
Honeybees	_____ _____ _____
Leafcutter ants and honeybees	_____ _____

7 Minibeast Homes

← Read pages 16–17.

1 Use the code to write the minibeasts. Then write the numbers.

a	d	e	f	g	h	i	l	m	n	o	p	r	s	t	w	y
★	≋	⊙	←	⇔	•	⊕	❖	⊡	✿	▲	☼	□	⊿	◆	+	O

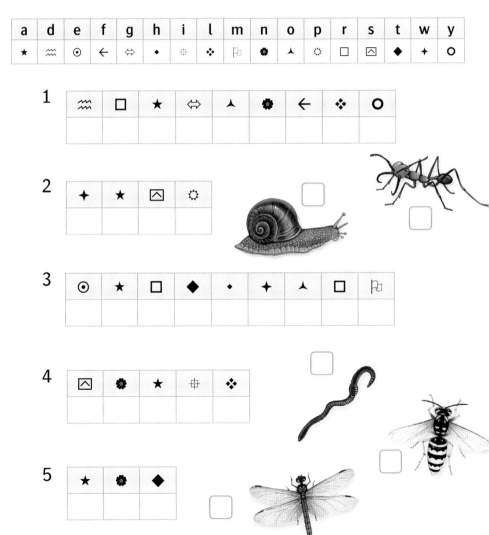

1 | ≋ | □ | ★ | ⇔ | ▲ | ✿ | ← | ❖ | O |

2 | + | ★ | ⊿ | ☼ |

3 | ⊙ | ★ | □ | ◆ | • | + | ▲ | □ | ⊡ |

4 | ⊿ | ✿ | ★ | ⊕ | ❖ |

5 | ★ | ✿ | ◆ |

2 Write the words.

snail   dragonfly   ant   wasp

1 It's an insect that lives underground. _____

2 Its larvae live underwater. _____

3 It carries its home on its back. _____

4 It makes fantastic nests. _____

3 Complete the sentences.

paper   nests   queen   larvae   saliva

1 Lots of minibeasts make _____ .

2 Some wasps make nests from _____ .

3 Wasps make the paper from wood and _____ .

4 The _____ wasp lays eggs in the nest.

5 The wasp nest has lots of small rooms for the wasp _____ .

4 Answer the questions.

1 Which minibeasts live underground?

_____

2 Where do dragonflies lay their eggs?

_____

3 Where do wasps live?

_____

8 Spiders

← Read pages 18–19.

1 **Write the words.**

spider web leaves
poison mice liquid

 1 _____

 2 _____

 3 _____

4 _____ 5 _____ 6 _____

2 **Write the words in order. Then write *true* or *false*.**

1 spiders / silk. / All / make / can

   All spiders can make silk. _____

2 webs. / spiders / make / All

   _____ _____

3 hunt. / spiders / All

   _____ _____

4 spider / makes / a / The / web. / wolf

   _____ _____

5 wolf / mice. / The / eats / spider

   _____ _____

3 Complete the chart.

	Spiders	Insects
How many body parts?	_____	_____
How many legs?	_____	_____
How many eyes?	_____ _____ _____	Some have two eyes and some also have extra eyes.
What food do they eat?	_____ _____	_____ _____
What can they make?	_____ _____	_____ _____

4 Draw and write about spiders.

Spiders have _____

_____

_____

They can _____

_____

⑨ Problems with Minibeasts

← Read pages 20–21.

ant   mosquito   locust
beetle   moth

1 **Write the words.**

1 _____   2 _____   3 _____

4 _____   5 _____

2 **Circle the correct words.**

1 A wasp can sting **again** and **again** / **only once**.

2 **All** / **Some** spiders have a poisonous bite.

3 A person **can** / **can't** die from the bite of a black widow spider.

4 **Spiders** / **Mosquitoes** give people malaria.

5 **Male** / **Female** mosquitoes bite.

6 Locusts eat **food crops** / **clothes**.

3 **Find and write the minibeast.**

It doesn't eat food crops.

It doesn't eat clothes.

It doesn't eat furniture.

It doesn't have eight legs.

It doesn't sting and then die.

bee	beetle
spider	~~locust~~
mosquito	moth

It's a _____

4 **Write about minibeasts that you like and don't like.**

I like _____ because_____

_____

_____

I like _____ because_____

_____

_____

I don't like _____ because_____

_____

_____

I don't like _____ because_____

_____

_____

10 Useful Minibeasts

← Read pages 22–23.

1 Write the minibeasts and other animals.

g^ro^f   ta^b   _shi^f

1 _____   2 _____   3 _____

k^or^m_wi^l_s   ^th_er_wo_r_am   ^e_be

4 _____   5 _____   6 _____

2 Match. Then write the sentences.

Fish, frogs, and bats ——┐   let air and water into soil.

Silkworms   └—— eat minibeasts.

Earthworms   give us honey.

Bees   give us silk.

Insects   move pollen from flower
                           to flower.

1 Fish, frogs, and bats eat minibeasts.

2 _____

3 _____

4 _____

5 _____

3 **Write about minibeasts.**

Problems with minibeasts:

They can sting. _____

_____

_____

_____

Good things about minibeasts:

Bees give us honey. _____

_____

_____

_____

4 **Can you remember? Which minibeast is it?**

1 It tastes with its feet. _____

2 They communicate with light. _____

3 It carries its home. _____

4 It makes nests with wood and saliva. _____

5 It eats fungus. _____

6 Its larvae live underwater. _____

7 It carries its baby on its back. _____

8 It has four legs on each section. _____

9 It can only eat liquids. _____

10 It can give people malaria. _____

Counting Minibeasts

1 Draw and write the minibeasts that you see in five days.

Days	Minibeasts
Monday	
Tuesday	
Wednesday	
Thursday	
Friday	

2 Count the minibeasts. Draw a graph.

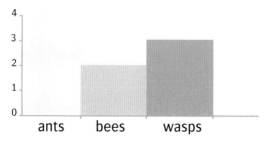

3 Display your graph.

Project 2 Minibeasts in My Country

1   Write the minibeasts that you can see in your country.

Minibeasts in the House

_____
_____
_____

Minibeasts in the Park

_____
_____
_____

Minibeasts in Water

_____
_____
_____

2   Draw ☺ next to the minibeasts that you like.

3   Write about the minibeasts that you like.

4   Display your work.

Picture Dictionary

 backbone

 bite

 bone

 clothes

 crops

 dark

 desert

 die

 female

 food

 forest

 fungus

 grow

 hide

 honey

 leaves

 liquid

 male

 mice

 mountain

move up
and down

nectar

ocean

parents

plants

poison

roots

saliva

scientist

seeds

silk

smell

soil

sound

sting

taste

tongue

touch

underground

wood

Oxford Read and Discover

Series Editor: Hazel Geatches • CLIL Adviser: John Clegg

Oxford Read and Discover graded readers are at four levels, from 3 to 6, suitable for students from age 8 and older. They cover many topics within three subject areas, and can support English across the curriculum, or Content and Language Integrated Learning (CLIL).

Available for each reader:
• Activity Book
• Audio CD Pack (book & audio CD)

For Teacher's Notes & CLIL Guidance go to
www.oup.com/elt/teacher/readanddiscover

Subject Area / Level	The World of Science & Technology	The Natural World	The World of Arts & Social Studies
3 600 headwords	• Super Structures • Your Five Senses • How We Make Products • Sound and Music	• Amazing Minibeasts • Wonderful Water • All About Rainforest Life • Animals In the Air	• Free Time Around the World • Festivals Around the World
4 750 headwords	• All About Plants • Machines Then and Now • Keeping Fit and Healthy • Recycle, Recycle, Recycle	• All About Ocean Life • Incredible Earth • All About Desert Life • Animals In the Night	• Wonders Of the Past • Animals In Art
5 900 headwords	• Transportation Then and Now • Wild Weather • Materials To Products • Medicine Then and Now	• Great Migrations • Exploring Our World • Animal Life Cycles • Life On Islands	• Homes Around the World • Our World In Art
6 1,050 headwords	• Clothes Then and Now • Your Amazing Body • Cells and Microbes • Incredible Energy	• All About Space • Caring For Our Planet • Earth Then and Now • Wonderful Ecosystems	• Food Around the World • Helping Around the World

Oxford Read and Discover readers shown in GRAY available early 2011.
For younger students, **Dolphin Readers** Levels Starter, 1, and 2 are available.